GREAT **KIWI** SLANG

GREAT
KIWI
SLANG

Compiled by
Sonya Plowman

SUMMIT
PRESS

PRESS

Unit 11/101–111 Diana Drive
Glenfield, Auckland 10
New Zealand
Phone: +64 9444 4144
Fax: +64 9444 4518
Email: publishing@fivemile.com.au

First published 2002

Editor: Samone Bos
Cover design: Diana Vlad
Text design: R.T.J. Klinkhamer
Cartoons: Geoff Hocking

Printed in Australia by Griffin Press

National Library of Australia
Cataloguing-in-Publication data

1. English language - New Zealand - Slang - Dictionaries.
I. Plowman, Sonya, 1972– .
427.993

ISBN 1 86503 667 6

Contents

Introduction

If you think that the Kiwis have slang down to a fine art, well you ain't wrong, bro. Contained within are some of New Zealand's most colourful words and phrases. Some might make you feel like tossing your lollies, but blimmin eck, it's a good read.

Of course, no slang dictionary would be complete without addressing the range of insults used in everyday life. If you're trying to find just the right expression to tell a dunce, a wacko, or someone who's shickered, shellacked and shit-faced to bugger off, you've come to the right place. So get your 'a' into 'g' and read on!

Sonya Plowman

Kiwi Slang from

ab-fab
absolutely fabulous.

ace, upon one's
alone, as in 'He was on his ace, walking sorrowfully down the road.'

acid
pressure, as in 'He put the acid on me to lend him some money.'

acre
a euphemism for buttocks, as in 'Get off your bloody acre and do something!'

across the ditch
Australia.

act the goat
silly, raucous behaviour.

afghan
a biscuit deriving its name from its cocoa colouring.

after match function
> a boozy get-together, usually after a team sporting match, and commonly involving only males.

afto, arvo
> afternoon.

aggro
> to describe an aggressive person.

'a' into 'g', to get one's
> arse into gear, an admonishment to hurry up, as in 'Get your 'a' into 'g' and get in the car!'

alchie
> alcoholic.

allakufic
> a quick, less-offensive way of saying 'Couldn't give a f***'.

all around the pig's arse there is pork
> stating the obvious, akin to the phrase 'Does a bear shit in the woods?'

All Blacks
> the national rugby team of New Zealand.

all cock and ribs (like a musterer's dog)
> very thin animal or person.

alley up
> to pay back (a debt).

*all hair oil and
no socks*
    someone who appears
    flashy but offers little
    of value.

all hands and the cook
    everybody.

*all hunched up like a
dog on a bag of staples*
    to describe someone who
    looks very uncomfortable.

*all over the place
like a madwoman's
breakfast*
    to describe the actions of a sportsperson who is
    falling below par.

all piss and wind
    boastful.

All Whites
    the national soccer team of New Zealand.

aluminium rain
    metal and other debris from a mid-air crash.

amber fluid, amber liquid
    beer.

amber gambler
    a driver who goes through the amber light at
    an intersection.

American tank
    a large American sedan.

ankle biter
    a fond and sometimes not-so-
    fond term for a small
    child or toddler.

Anzac Day dinner
    an Anzac Day 'liquid lunch'.

Anzac shandy
    champagne and beer.

'a' over 'k'
    arse over kite, a rough fall, as in 'He skidded
    on the ice and SPLAT! He went 'a' over 'k'.'

appetite like a fantail
    small, birdlike appetite.

apples
    an expression of optimism, usually used in the
    form 'she'll be apples'.

argue the toss
    to dispute a decision.

aroha job
work done free for love, from the Maori word aroha meaning 'love, fellow feeling'.

around the twist
insane.

arse around
to fool around.

arsehole
a despicable person, as in 'That bloke's a real arsehole.'

arsehole to breakfast, from
totality, as in 'He knows V8s from arsehole to breakfast.'

arse licker
a sycophant.

arse over tit
to fall down in a most undignified manner.

arse paper
useless person or thing.

arsey-boo
a mess.

Arthur or Martha, (doesn't know whether he's)
    to describe a confused, frazzled person.

as
    used to add weight to a statement, as in 'He downed a whole bottle of vodka and got as plastered as.'

as cold as a stepmother's kiss
    extremely cold.

as flat as a strap
    a flat area.

as long as his/her arse points to the ground
    indefinitely.

as low as whale shit
    a person with no redeeming qualities whatsoever.

as much chance of pushing shit uphill with a rubber fork
    no chance whatsoever.

ate the cow and worried the tail
    leftovers.

Auks, The
    Auckland's rugby team (more commonly known as The Blues).

auntie
a derogatory name for a suspected male homosexual.

Aussie
an Australian.

Aussie haka
the patting of breast and trouser pockets when it comes time to shout the next round at the pub (as a means of avoiding having to pay).

Aussie salute
the flapping away of ever-present flies from one's face.

away laughing
on the way to success; said of something that is easy to achieve, as in 'Now that Rangi's joined the team, we're away laughing.'

away with the fairies
said of someone who is daydreaming or not paying attention.

axe-handle
a measure of breadth, commonly of a woman's buttocks or a man's shoulders.

Backbone of the country BAH!

babbling brook
rhyming slang for cook.

bach
a humble weekend cottage; to live alone as a bachelor.

bachelorise
the act of a male coping when his female partner is away.

backblocker
an uncivilised person living in a remote place.

backblocks
a remote place.

backbone of the country
farmers.

backdoor bandit
a derogatory term for a homosexual man.

back of beyond
a remote place.

baffle with bull shit
  to lie or deceive.

bag
  to put someone or something down.

bagful of busted arseholes
  an ugly person or undesirable state, as in 'After
  all that booze last night I feel like a bagful of
  busted arseholes.'

ball, (up with the)
  in touch with the latest developments.

ball and chain
  sexist term for wife.

balls up
  to make a mess of things; a disastrous and
  often embarrassing mistake or gaff.

bandicooting
  surreptitiously stealing root vegetables, such as
  potatoes.

bang, (go out with a)
said of a successful occasion.

banged up
vulgar term for being pregnant.

banger
an impressive firecracker.

bang on
spot on, exactly right.

bangs like a dunny door in a high wind
said of a sexually enthusiastic person.

banjo
tackle to the head.

barber's cat, (all piss and wind like the)
utterly useless.

barbie/barby
barbeque.

bare-bottom haka
a dance which includes flashing one's buttocks
to another as a sign of contempt.

bark
to vomit.

barker's egg
dog shit.

barker's nest
a pile of dog shit.

barney
a rowdy argument or fight.

barrack
to support vocally (usually a sports team).

barracouta
long and narrow crusty loaf of bread similar in appearance to the fish of the same name.

barrel-arse
a short, stubby person.

base bludger/walloper
derogatory term for a military officer serving at the base.

bash
difficult travel through dense undergrowth, as in 'The short-cut meant they had to do some bush bashing.' Also a big party or drinking session.

bash, give something a
to try something ambitious.

bash up
to make something quickly or haphazardly.

Basin, The
a famous cricket ground in Wellington.

basket case
  a mentally deficient or anxious person.

bastard
  an unpleasant person; an affectionate
  appellation, as in 'What have you been up to,
  you old bastard?'

bathers
  swimwear.

← Bathers

battler
  one who doggedly works through grim times.

beach
  the seaside.

beat about the bush
     prevaricate.

beat the living daylights out of
     to administer a violent thrashing.

beaut
     excellent; a word of praise or approval.

beauty
     anything to one's liking, as in 'You little
     beauty!'

Beehive, The
     Wellington's parliament building.

beer gut
     a man's bulging stomach, often associated with
     heavy drinking.

beer sandwich
     liquid lunch.

bee's knees
     the best.

belly buster
     a badly executed dive whereupon the diver
     lands on his or her belly.

belt
     a stiff drink.

bench
     the seat on which rugby reserves sit.

bender
   a derogatory term for a Catholic.

bend the elbow
   to drink excessively, as in 'I hear he bends the elbow a bit.'

benedict
   a newly married man, one who had previously been considered a confirmed bachelor.

berko, berkers
   a person who becomes very violent or emotional, as in 'Jay went berko when his car was stolen.'

better than a poke up the arse with a burnt stick
   not so bad; an admission that things could be worse.

bet your balls
   a guarantee, as in 'Bet your balls he doesn't get to go home with her tonight.'

Bible-banger, Bible-basher, Bible-thumper
   a preacher or religious person who preaches excessively.

biff out
> to throw out.

big ask
> a lot to expect, as in 'Driving you all the way out to the airport from here? That's a big ask, isn't it?'

big bickies
> lots of money.

biggie
> euphemistic term for defecation.

big girl's blouse
> a timid or effeminate man.

big-note
> to act important; to boast.

big smoke, the
> a large town or city.

big spit
> vomit, or the act of vomiting.

big wraps on, to have
> highly rated.

bikie
> member of a motorbike gang.

billy
> tin can used as a container and cooking/boiling utensil.

billyo
> with great speed or gusto, as in 'The old bomb goes like billyo.'

binder
> a hearty meal.

binocs
> shortened form of binoculars.

bird
> easy; to make a success of.

bite on, to put the
> to ask for a loan.

bitser
> a mongrel dog.

biv, bivvy
> short form of bivouac - a temporary shelter.

bizzo
> business.

BJ
> blowjob.

black budget
> a severe and unpopular budget.

Black Caps
> nickname of the New Zealand representative cricket eleven.

Black Ferns
the New Zealand women's rugby team.

blackman
treacle.

Black Stump
An undefinable and non-existent place in remote areas, as in 'It's out somewhere this side of the Black Stump.'

Blenheimers
memory loss as a result from drinking too much wine.

blimey, Charlie!
an expression of relief or surprise.

blimmin, blimmin eck
a polite alternative to bloody.

blind
extremely intoxicated.

blinded with science
overwhelmed with a mass of detail.

blister
a strong, written reprimand.

block, do your
to lose your temper.

bloke
fellow, man.

bloody hell
all-purpose
expletive.

bloody oath
an affirmative; you bet!

blow a fuse
to lose one's temper.

blowie
blowfly.

blow in
an unexpected
guest.

blow in the bag
    take a Breathalyser test for alcohol
    consumption.

blow that for a joke
    the dismissal of a suggestion; an expression
    showing exasperation.

blow through
    to pass through a place without stopping.

bludge
    to live off others; to loaf on the job.

blue
    a brawl; a mistake; a red-haired person.

blue duck
    a lost cause; a failure.

blue fit
    to be very angry or shocked, as in 'After she
    found out what her son had done, she ran
    around in a blue fit.'

blue lady
    methylated spirits.

blue rinse brigade
    older, wealthy women who put blue rinses
    through their hair.

blue-veiner
    vulgar term for penis.

bluey
nickname often given to blokes with red hair; notice of a court summons.

boatie
someone who operates a small boat.

bob each way, to have a
hedging one's bets.

bobsy-die
a fuss.

Bob's your uncle
that's all there is to it, as in 'Just nail that in there and Bob's your uncle.'

bodgie
something of dubious quality.

bogan
a misfit.

bog in
to set to work with vigour, often used in reference to starting a meal.

boiled dog
an affectation; the act of putting on airs and graces.

boilover
a surprising or unexpected result.

bolter
a (usually successful) outsider, commonly in the racehorse or footrace context.

bomb
something dilapidated, often in reference to cars.

Bombay bloomers
baggy, loose shorts.

bone people
derogatory term for middle-class white people who wear carved bone jewellery in solidarity with the Maoris.

boner
vulgar term for an erect penis.

bonza/bonzer
something that is pleasing or of good quality.

boob tatt
a tattoo acquired in jail.

boohai
a remote location.

boomer
anything large or first-rate.

boots and all
with total commitment.

booze artist
an alcoholic.

boozer
a heavy drinker; the local pub.

boozerooster
a drunkard.

bo-peep
a look; a peep.

borax
banter.

bore the pants off (someone), to
to be excessively boring.

bot
a bug or germ, as in 'She's caught the bot, so you better keep away from her.'

bottler
someone or something that is excellent.

botty
chesty, as in 'She's come down with a botty cough.'

bowldacks
bull shit.

bow tie
the boyfriend of a married woman.

box
vulgar term for female genitals.

boxed up
lost or confused.

box of birds
fit and happy, as in 'How ya going, mate? Box of birds?' 'Yep, box of birds, mate.'

box of fluffies
    healthy and happy, as in 'How ya going, mate?
    Box of fluffies?' 'Yep, box of fluffies, mate.'

box on
    to persevere, as in 'I'll box on with it and try
    to finish before midnight.'

box seat
    the best place to be.

boys in blue
    police.

boys on the hill
    members of parliament.

brass razoo
    a small amount of money, usually expressed
    negatively, as in 'Mate, I haven't got a brass
    razoo'.

break it down
    command akin to 'Stop that' or 'Take it easy'.

breather
    a short rest.

brekkie
    breakfast.

brew
    tea, coffee or an alcoholic beverage.

brewer's asthma
a hangover.

brewer's goitre
a beer gut.

brick short of a load, a
a simpleton.

DOH!

bride's nightie, off like a
to make a hasty departure.

bright spark
    a cheerful, alert person.

bro
    an affectionate abbreviation of brother, largely
    adopted by young Maoris and used amongst
    their mates.

broken-arse
    a prisoner who has buckled under the system
    and who has fallen to the bottom of the
    pecking order.

brown eye
    vulgar term for anus.

brown nose
    to crawl to someone; to be obsequious.

buck
    to object.

bucket
    severe criticism.

buck in
    to help for the good of all.

Buckley's/Buckley's chance
    very little or no chance.

buckshee
    something free; a welcome extra.

buggalugs
mate, as in, 'G'day buggalugs, how ya goin'?'

bugger all
very little; nothing.

buggered if I know
to have no idea.

buggerise about
muck about.

bugger me sideways
expression of surprise or disbelief.

bugger off
go away.

bugger that for a game of soldiers
expressing disapproval.

built like a brick shithouse
pertaining to a large and very muscular person.

bull shit artist
one who lies.

bull's roar
nowhere near; not even close.

bull's wool
slightly more polite term for bull shit.

bummer
disappointing event or turn of circumstance.

bun, to do your
to lose one's temper.

bun in the oven
coarse expression for being pregnant.

bung
broken, as in 'My bung leg's no good for
playing rugby.'

bung it on
to exaggerate.

bunk
truancy; to wag school.

burl, to give it a
to give it a go.

burn off, to
leave someone behind; make a hasty departure.

burnt stump, to stand out like a
to stand still, doing nothing.

burst, on the
making a vigorous advance through the
opposition (rugby).

bush Baptist
a person who tends to preach his strong
religious views.

bush carpenter
a carpenter with no formal training.

bushed
very tired or lost.

bush happy
a person who has become eccentric from living
alone too long.

bushie
bushman.

bush telegraph
the gossip grapevine.

bushwhacked
exhausted.

bust your boiler, to
over-exert oneself.

busy as a bee with a bumful of honey
extremely busy.

BUTA
  'boot up the arse'.

butcher's, to not give a
  to not care, as in 'So long as the hotel's clean I
  don't give a butcher's how much it costs.'

buttinski
  to butt in.

buzz around like a bee in a bottle
  busy or confused.

BYO
  bring your own (usually alcohol).

By (pai, py) korry
  exclamation,
  euphemism for
  by God.

C

cab sav
abbreviation of cabernet sauvignon.

cack-handed
left-handed; clumsy.

cactus
trouble, as in 'I'm in the cactus.'

cake hole
mouth.

call Ralph
to vomit.

can-a-piss
can of beer.

Captain Cooker
New Zealand wild pig.

carbie
shortened form of carburettor.

cardie
shortened form of cardigan.

cark
to die.

carn
come on!

cashie
illegal tax-free cash.

caught short
having no money at bill time; a desperate need to go to the toilet (usually without a toilet available).

charge like a wounded bull
to set excessively high prices.

chateau cardboard
cheap bulk wine in a cask.

chew the fat
to chat, natter.

chiack
to tease or jeer.

chilly bin
sealable, insulated box which keeps food and drink cold.

Chinese burn
the twisting of wrist or leg skin between two hands.

chippie
potato chip; carpenter.

chocka
full, overflowing.

choice!
exclamation of approval.

choke a darkie
vulgar term for defecation.

chookie
girlfriend; young woman.

Firm breasts

Hello ducks!

Hiyachooksie

Firm thighs

chook's mouth
 the mouth.

choppers
 teeth.

Chrissy
 shortened form of Christmas.

Christchurch!
 an alternative interjection for damn.

chrome dome
 a derogatory term for a bald person.

chuck
 throw; vomit.

chuck a U-ie
 to make a U-turn whilst driving.

chuck a wobbly
 to throw a tantrum.

chuck up
 to vomit.

chuddy/chuddy-gum
 chewing-gum.

chunder
 to vomit.

chute, up the
 awry; in serious trouble.

ciggie
shortened form of cigarette.

City of Sails
Auckland.

Clayton's
a substitute for the real thing, as in 'I can't afford a genuine Gucci watch, so I got a Clayton's one from Bali.'

clean up
defeat, particularly in reference to sport.

climb into
to severely criticise someone.

climb the wall
to go mad.

clock
to punch, as in 'I clocked him in the head'.

clued up
well-informed.

coathanger/kotanga
car aerial.

cobber
> a mate, friend.

cockie/cocky
> a small farmer (pertains to a cockatoo scratching at a patch of dirt).

cold enough to freeze the balls off a brass monkey
> extremely cold.

colder than a mother-in-law's kiss
> very unfriendly.

colly wobbles
> feeling extremely nervous, sometimes to the point of feeling nauseous.

come at
> to refuse to consider, as in 'She won't come at the idea of lending me any more money.'

come a thud
> a failure.

come good
> recovery after a setback, as in 'My leg's come good now that I've been seeing the physiotherapist.'

come to light with
> to supply something, as in 'The landlord finally came to light with a new paint job.'

come up against
  to encounter trouble.

compo
  shortened form of workers' compensation.

con artist
  someone who deceives.

cooee, within
  close, as in 'He's within cooee of getting sacked.'

cooking with gas
  a solution, as in 'Once we get this tyre changed we're cooking with gas.'

cook the books
  to illegally falsify records or accounts.

cop
  to catch or capture.

cop ya later
  see you later (coarse play on the word copulate.)

corker
  something or someone considered to be excellent.

cot-case
  someone who is a candidate for admission to a lunatic asylum, often used in relation to excessive alcohol consumption.

cotton onto, to
> to understand; to attach oneself to another
> (possibly unwilling) person.

cough one's cud
> to vomit.

couldn't lie straight in bed
> a liar.

*couldn't win if he started the night
before*
> a slow racehorse or a hopeless individual.

cow
> a problematic thing or person, as in 'Putting
> this engine back together is a cow of a job.'

cow-banger/cow-cockie/cow-spanker
> a dairy farmer.

cow gravy/cow pat
> freshly deposited (or very soft) cow muck.

crack a fat
> vulgar term for an erection.

cracker
> rated very highly, as in 'That's a cracker TV
> you've got.'

crack hardy/hearty
> to put on a brave front.

crack it
to succeed.

crack on about
to talk on and on.

crack the whip
to take one's turn.

crash hot
first rate.

crawler
a sycophant.

LICK !

cream
to convincingly win a sporting match.

crib
a holiday cottage in the South Island.

crim
shortened form of criminal.

croak
to die.

crook
unwell, angry or dishonest.

crook, to go
to display anger, as in 'You should have seen him go crook at me when I broke the window.'

crown jewels, the
male private parts.

crust
livelihood.

crustie
used by teenagers when referring to an old person.

cuff, a bit on the
to be unfair or too severe.

cunning as a shithouse rat
to be very sly or cunning.

cupful of cold sick
indicative of a poor performance, particularly in relation to sport.

cuppa
cup of tea (or coffee).

curly one
a difficult question, as in 'Will I ever get married again? Mate, that's a curly one!'

cushy
    well paid,
    undemanding
    (of a job).

custard, to
turn
    said of a plan
    or relationship
    that has soured.

cut a track
    to depart, usually in haste.

cut cat, to go like a
    indicative of a hasty retreat, as in 'When he
    saw us coming he ran
    like a cut cat.'

cut the cheese
    to fart.

cuz
    shortened
    form of
    cousin.

dacks/daks
men's trousers.

dag
affectionate term for a person who is funny
without pretence; also used to describe a
person with no interest in fashion.

dairy
a corner store selling a variety of groceries.

dance a haka
a phrase indicating pleasure, as in 'When
Ranji's horse came in first he danced a haka.'

dark on
to be angry about something, as in 'Mum was really dark on Dad when he didn't come home in time for dinner.'

dash
very small amount of liquid, as in 'Add a dash of rum to my glass.'

date
vulgar term for anus.

daylight robbery
the excessive overcharging for goods or services.

dead as a moa
long dead.

deadbeat
a person who is down on their luck.

deadman's arm
a leg of lamb.

dead ringer
very close likeness, as in 'Mate, you're a dead ringer for your brother.'

dead spit of
   very close likeness.

dead to the world
   in a deep, possibly alcohol-induced sleep.

deal to
   to treat someone roughly.

decko
   a look, as in 'Take a decko at that chick in the mini skirt!'

delish/delishimo
   delicious.

demon
   a detective.

dero/derro
   a derelict person, usually living on the street.

dick
   to lose, as in 'They were dicked by those guys over there.'

dickhead/dickwhacker
   an idiot.

dicky
   uncertain, risky.

didn't come down in the last shower
shrewd, quick witted.

diff
difference, as in 'What's the diff?'

diffy
shortened form for the differential of a vehicle.

dig deep
a mighty effort.

digger
greeting used between males; a name for a
New Zealand or Australian returned
serviceman.

dig in
to work energetically; to start eating.

dillbrain
stupid or silly person.

dindins
dinner.

ding
a dent in a car.

dingbat
a crazy person.

dingo
an Australian.

dinkum Kiwi
a person considered to be quintessentially of New Zealand.

dinky
small or cute.

dinky-di
true, fair, honest.

dip one's lid
to raise one's hat and lower one's head in respect.

dip out of
to miss out on something; to fail.

dip south
to search pockets for money.

dirt-tracker
a mid-week player for the All Blacks.

dirty big
extremely big.

dirty on
upset or angry, as in 'She was dirty on me after I broke up with her.'

dirty play
unfair sporting practices.

dish licker
    dog.

ditch
    the Tasman Sea,
    particularly used in
    reference to Australia.

dividend/divvy
    a pay out from the
    TAB.

*do a moonlight
flit, to*
    to leave at night
    without paying a
    debt.

dob in
    to tell on someone.

doctor, to go for
    to make a supreme effort to win.

doesn't give a bugger, she/he
used to describe someone who could not care less.

doesn't miss a trick, she/he
used to describe a very alert person.

dogbox, in the
to be in trouble, particularly with one's wife.

dog's breakfast
a mess.

dog tucker
defeated.

dole bludger
someone who lives on Social Security benefits instead of getting a job.

do me a favour
a remark indicating that you want another person to desist from his/her comments.

domestic
family disagreement, usually between husband and wife.

done like a dog's dinner
well and truly defeated.

dong, donger
vulgar term for penis.

donkey
a useless racehorse.

donkey-deep, to be in
to be in serious trouble.

donkey lick
to defeat decisively.

doodackie, a
an item that's name can't be thought of.

doodackied up
spruced up.

doolan
an Irish Catholic.

do one's dough, to
to spend all of one's money.

do over
to treat someone roughly or dishonestly.

do-ray-me
money.

dorkbrain
imbecile.

Dorklander
Aucklander.

dosh
money.

doss down
   to find a rough-and-ready place to spend the
   night.

do the dirty, to
   to do the wrong thing by someone.

double
   to carry a passenger on a bicycle.

doughnut
   a tight circle driven by a car, often performed
   by louts.

down south
   somewhere on the South Island.

down the coast diving for fish farts
   a description of someone's dead-end job, as in
   'He left school a year early and now he's down
   the coast diving for fish farts.'

down the road
   dismissal from work, as in 'He stole some stuff
   from work so he was sent down the road.'

down to the wire
   a very close competition with the winner not
   becoming clear until the very end.

down trou
   the lowering of trousers to shock or amuse.

do your dough
   to waste all your money.

DPB
the Domestic
Purposes Benefit.

drag the chain
to be the
slowest
drinker in the
pub.

drain the dragon
(of a man) to urinate.

drive the pigs home
to snore.

drongo
a stupid and clumsy fool.

drop
to break off a
relationship with a
boyfriend or girlfriend.

drop in it
to get someone into trouble.

dropkick
a despicable or disliked person.

drop off the perch
to die.

drop one's bundle
to throw a hissy fit; to lose one's temper.

droppie
a dropkick or dropped field goal in rugby
union football.

drum
correct information, as in 'Rangi's got the
drum on the weather report.'

dry horrors
suffering alcoholic dehydration.

duck shove
avoid responsibility; to pass the buck.

dump one's load
vulgar term for ejaculation.

dunny
toilet, especially an outside toilet.

dunny diver
a plumber.

durry
a roll-your-own variety of cigarette.

dust up
a fight or brawl.

dyke
a toilet.

E

earbash

to talk incessantly to a
person who is not
interested in what
you are saying.

early shower, to take an
  to be sent off the field during a game because
  of foul play.

earwig
  an eavesdropper; to eavesdrop.

*easy as shoving a slab of butter up a
cow's bum with a size five knitting
needle on a hot day, as*
  very difficult.

egg beater
  helicopter.

eh?
  rhetorical interrogative expressed at the end of
  sentences.

electric puha
  marijuana.

emu parade
  the act of picking up rubbish in the school
  yard as punishment.

engine room
  rugby nickname for the 'tight five' forwards.

enough to choke a bull
  a substantial money roll.

Enzed
  New Zealand.

Enzedder
a New Zealander.

euchred
defeated.

even-Stevens
an equal chance or amount.

ever thought of renting your mouth out for a car park?
said to a loud mouth.

every man and his dog
a great crowd of people; a wide cross-section of society.

everything but the cat's blanket
a supreme effort.

extra
said as emphasis, as in 'Ranji's missus is extra good-looking.'

eyes out, to go
to go at top speed.

face fart
to belch.

face like a bull's bum
exceedingly ugly.

fag
cigarette.

fag hag
derogatory term for a female who is friends with male homosexuals.

fair cow
a disagreeable thing or event.

fair crack of the whip/fair suck of the sav
an appeal for fairness.

fair dinkum
    truly.

fair enough
    expression used to concede a point.

fakawi?
    abbreviated form of 'Where the f*** are we?'

fart-arsing about
    messing around.

fart sack
    sleeping bag.

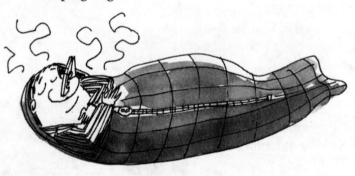

fat
    vulgar term for an erection.

fat show
    no chance.

feed
    a good, satisfying meal.

feed a line
to lie or give misleading information.

fern leaf
a New Zealander.

few
a shortened form for a few beers, as in 'Let me just sink a few before we get to the party.'

financial
having a fair bit of money on one's person or in the bank.

fine art, to have something down to a
to be skilled at something, commonly associated with illegal activities.

fire in the fern
trouble looming.

firing blanks
vulgar term for being unable to impregnate a woman.

fish hooks
difficulties.

fit as a buck rat, as
a very fit person.

fit up
to find or fabricate evidence.

fizz-boat
  a small motor boat.

fizzer
  a failure or fiasco.

fizzy drink
  soft drink.

flag away
  to give something up.

flakers
  unconscious through having too much alcohol.

flash a brown
  to pull one's pants down and flash the
  buttocks.

flash as a rat with a gold tooth
ostentatious; tastelessly overdressed.

flat to the boards
extreme effort, as in 'I was going flat to the
boards to get everything done by six.'

flax-bag terrorist
a derogatory name for a Maori activist.

flick one's wick
to hurry up.

flip your lid
to become angry.

floater
a turd that won't flush down the toilet.

float up to
to casually approach a person or group.

flog
to steal.

flog the log
vulgar term for masturbation.

flophouse
a cheap boarding house; accommodation for
homeless men.

fluff
a soft-sounding and very smelly fart.

fly cemetery
fruit loaf.

folding stuff
paper money.

fong
alcohol.

footy
rugby or rugby league.

for crying out loud
an expression of annoyance.

freckle
  vulgar term for anus.

Frenchie/Frenchy
  a condom.

front bum
  vulgar term for vagina.

f***-knuckle/f***wit
  an idiot.

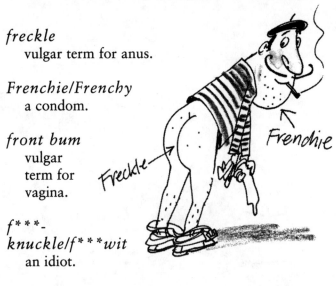

full of beans
  frisky, energetic.

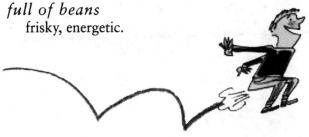

full tit
  to go full speed.

fun bags
  breasts.

FY boots
  'F*** you' boots, a somewhat slutty variety of boots.

garbiologist
    a garbage collector.

gargle
    a drink.

gate
    mouth, as in 'I'll punch you in the gate if you
    don't shut it!'

g'day
   standard greeting.

gear
   clothes, as in 'Get your gear on and come outside.'

geeza
   a look, as in 'C'mon, give us a geeza!'

gekko
   a look.

get a boot out of
   to gain pleasure from something.

get down on
   to steal.

get in behind
   a command to do as you are told.

get it on with
   to have an affair or sexual liaison with someone.

get off the grass
   expression of disbelief or disapproval.

get on your goat
   to annoy, irritate.

get your goat

get out of jail
    to be very lucky.

get plunked
    vulgar term for becoming pregnant.

get stuck into
    to start eating; to fight.

get the old heave-ho
    to be fired.

gink
    a look or glimpse.

girl's blouse
    to be weak, passive.

give it a burl
    to try something.

give it away
    a command to abandon an idea.

give it heaps
    to try hard; to make fun of someone.

gizza
    shortened form of 'give us a...'

glutton for punishment
    said of someone who willingly takes on
    unpleasant tasks or frequently gets into
    unfortunate situations.

God botherer.
a religious maniac.

go down the gurgler
to go bankrupt, out
of business or to have
a plan ruined.

Godzone
New Zealand.

go in boots and all
to have total
enthusiasm.

going bush
getting away from
city life.

go like a strangled fart
to move slowly.

go like the clappers
to work or move extremely fast.

go much on
to approve of, commonly used in negative
constructions, as in 'I don't go much on the
boss's way of doing things.'

goobie
a gob of spit or phlegm.

good keen man.
  a decent back-country bloke.

good-oh
  statement of agreement.

good on ya
  words of encouragement or praise, akin to
  'Good for you!'

good wicket
  good state to be in, as in 'We'll soon be on a
  good wicket with this money rolling in.'

go off at
  to admonish.

goog
  an egg.

go on
  an exclamation showing disbelief or doubt, as
  in 'You really proposed to Sharon last night?
  Go on!'

goss
  gossip.

go the whole nine yards
  to give maximum effort.

go to buggery
  an unpleasant way to say go away, akin to 'go
  to Hell'.

go to the pack
  to deteriorate, as in 'His liver's gone to the pack since he started drinking again.'

graft
  hard manual labour.

Grand Scale Theft
  G.S.T.

graunch
  a loud grinding sound, often used in relation to not changing gears properly.

greaser
  a heavy fall, as in 'She slid on the ice and came a greaser!'

greasies
  take-away fast food, of the greasy variety.

greenie
  conservationist; environmentalist.

grog
  alcoholic beverages.

grogged up
  drunk.

groggery
  the pub.

grotty
  dirty, unsavoury.

grouse
  great, fine, excellent.

grunds/gruts
  underpants.

grunt
  power, as in 'Man, this
  car's got a lot of grunt.'

gumboot
  a condom.

*gumdigger's dog, as
stupid as a*
  very stupid.

gummie/gummy
  shortened form of
  gumboot.

gutful
  more than enough, as
  in 'I've had a gutful of
  your behaviour, young
  missy.'

guts for garters
  in big trouble, as in 'I'll have your
  bloody guts for garters if you
  don't clean up that mess right now!'

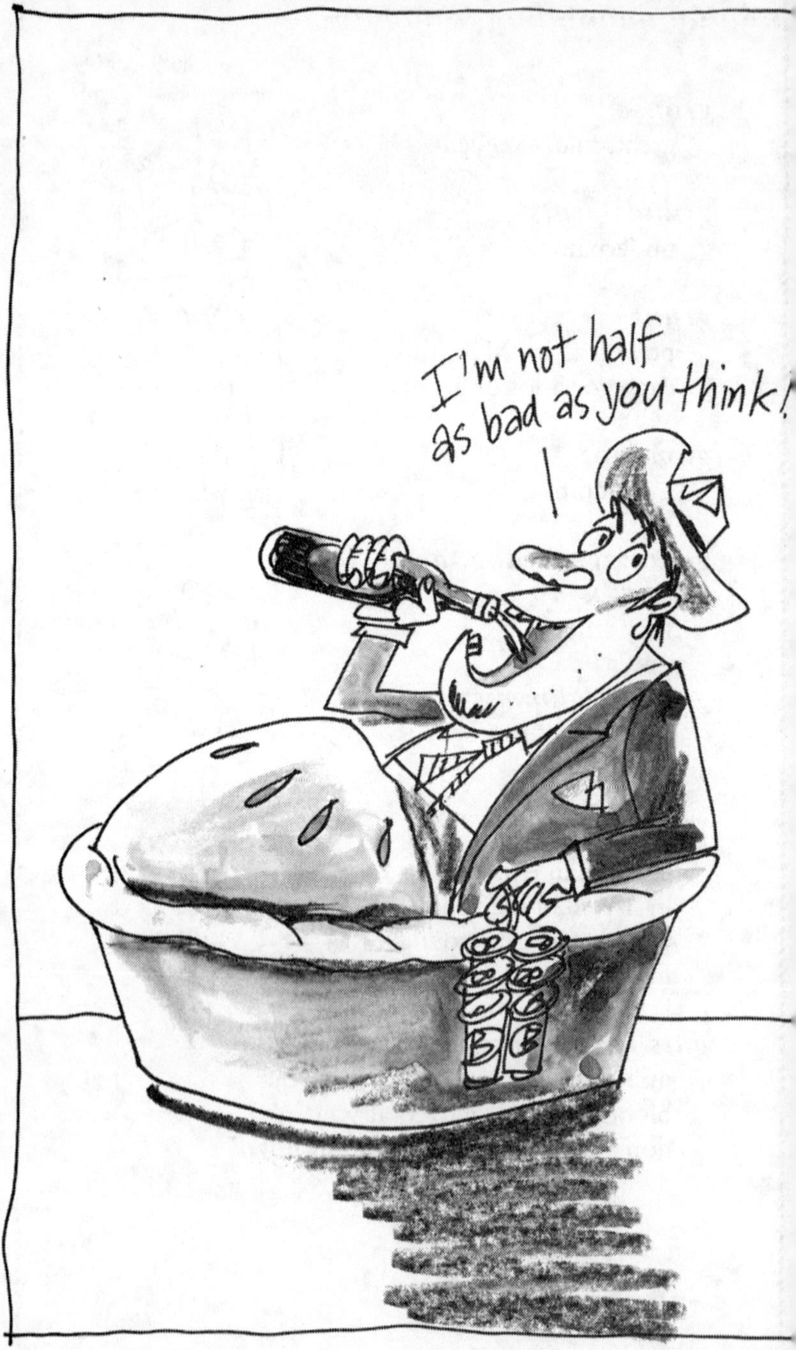
I'm not half
as bad as you think!

H

had it
exhaustion or exasperation, as in 'I've had it with this stupid essay!'

hairy
tricky, as in 'That's a pretty hairy question, mate.'

half a shake
just a moment, as in 'I'll be there in half a shake.'

half cut
on the way to being drunk.

half pie
incomplete or imperfect.

half your luck
expression indicating that you feel the other person is very fortunate.

hangava
polite substitute for helluva.

hangman
a hard case, as in 'The new foreman at work is a real hangman.'

happy as Larry
very happy or pleased.

hard as nails
in good condition.

hard case
joker, comedian.

hard word on, to put the
a demand for something, commonly money.

hasn't got a cracker
to be completely penniless.

have a slash
to urinate.

have a squat
to defecate.

have the goods on
holding incriminating evidence, as in 'I've got the goods on you; I know what you've been up to.'

having a colourful conversation with the big white telephone
throwing up down the toilet.

having a rottie
  in a very bad mood.

head down, arse up
  hard at work.

head over turkey
  falling over in a very inelegant manner.

head sherang
  the boss.

heap of shit
  useless thing.

heap shit on
>   tease or abuse, as in 'They heaped shit on him because he wore a dress.'

he, I'll go
>   a phrase showing confidence in a belief, as in 'If he's not hiding in here, I'll go he.'

herbs, to give it
>   power, as in 'Give it some herbs; see if that gets her going.'

hide the salami/sausage
>   vulgar term for sexual intercourse.

hit the sack
>   to go to bed.

hit the spot
>   to achieve the desired outcome. 'Ah, that nip of brandy really hit the spot.'

hit up
>   to inject with illicit drugs.

hit your straps
>   to depart hastily.

hobnail express
>   to go by foot.

hoe in
>   to attack vigorously.

hoick
to spit.

hokonui
illegal alcohol.

holding paddock
a nursing home for elderly people.

Hollywood, to throw a
to be a drama queen; to exaggerate the
seriousness of an injury (commonly during a
sporting match) to gain advantage.

home and hosed
safe and secure.

home on the pig's back
having arrived at success.

hoodackie/hoodickie
term for something that you don't know the
name for, akin to thingamebob.

hook one's bait
to depart.

hoon
a lout; a fast, reckless driver.

hooter
a nose.

hoover
to eat or drink everything in sight.

hop across
to make a quick or unexpected trip, usually of short duration.

hop up and down
to act in a very distressed manner.

hose off
to make someone angry.

hostile at, to go
to become angry with someone; to show someone you are mad, as in 'He became hostile at me when he found out what I'd done.'

how's your father
a fight, especially on the rugby field.

huckery
unpleasant or unwell.

hui-hopper
someone who attends meetings incessantly.

humdinger
anything thought to be terrific.

hunky dory
fine, as in 'How are ya, mate?' 'Hunky dory.'

hurl
  to vomit.

hydraulic sandwich
  a liquid lunch (usually beer).

hydroglycaemic as a newt, as
  drunk.

I didn't come down in the last shower
   to state that one is cluey, shrewd and quick-
   witted, not naive.

I don't give a rat's arse
   a show of complete indifference, as in 'I don't
   give a rat's arse that the boss wants to see me.'

if bull shit was music, you'd have your own orchestra
   said to someone talking nonsense.

if he laughed his face would crack
   said of a dour individual.

if it were raining palaces you'd be hit on the head by a dunny door
   said of an unlucky individual.

if it were raining virgins you'd be locked in the dunny with a poofter
   said of a very unlucky individual.

if you bought a kangaroo it wouldn't hop
> said of an exceedingly unlucky individual.

if you can't be good, be careful
> advice to take care, especially when about to go to a party.

if you think that, then you've got another thing coming
> said to someone who is very mistaken.

I'll be buggered/I'll be a monkey's uncle
> expression of surprise and amazement.

illegal tegel
> a protected bird taken illegally for food.

I'll hand it to him
    a reluctant expression of approval for someone
    for something they have accomplished.

*I'll knock your teeth so far down your
throat you'll have to stick a toothbrush
up your arse to clean them.*
    a subtle threat.

I'll see you right
    a promise to take care of someone, particularly
    in regards to financial assistance.

improve, on the
    getting better, in reference to an injury or
    illness.

in deep shit
in big trouble.

in for your chop
working hard to get your share.

in good nick
in good shape.

in the cactus
in trouble.

in the club
pregnant.

in the dogbox
in disgrace.

in the poo
in trouble.

investment
a bet on the races.

ironed out
exhausted or knocked
silly, usually as a
consequence of excessive
alcohol consumption or a physical fight.

iron undies
the bane of a frustrated male's existence: any
female underclothing that is difficult to get into
or take off.

it's moments like these you need Minties
an expression used in embarrassing situations
(taken from an advertising slogan).

I've seen better heads on a glass of beer
a statement that you're ugly.

I wouldn't piss on him if he was on fire
expression of contempt.

Jandals

jack
    to look, as in 'Take a jack at this!'

jack up
    to organise, support or increase.

JAFA
    Just Another F***in' Aucklander.

Jake, she'll be
    everything will be okay, as in 'Don't worry
    mate, once I get you to the hospital, she'll be
    Jake.'

jandal
    thong (footwear).

Jap crap
    supposedly poor quality goods from Japan.

jerkin' the gherkin
    vulgar term for male masturbation.

jerry
    to understand, as in 'She didn't jerry to the
    implications immediately; when she did, she
    knew she was in trouble.'

jiffy
a short period of time, as in 'I'm off to the dairy for a carton of milk - back in a jiffy.'

jigger
a small, manually-operated railway trolley used for transporting railway workers.

jiggered
broken or of no use.

jink
to cheat.

Joe
a silly person, as in 'You certainly made a Joe of yourself at the interview today.'

Joe Blow
the average bloke.

joker
a bloke.

judder bars
haemorrhoids.

jumbo
the buttocks.

jungle juice
strong alcohol.

junket trumpet
    vulgar term for penis.

just a mo
    a little bit more time, as in 'Hey Mac, I'll be
    with you in just a mo.'

just quietly
    in confidence, as in 'Just quietly, I think that
    guy's up to no good.'

just the berries
    exactly what is required, as in 'Ah, that slurp
    of rum was just the berries.'

K

kai
food.

kai cart
a fast-food cart or roadside takeaway.

kapai
excellent, fine, okay.

keepsies
for keeps.

kero
kerosene.

Khyber Pass
arse (rhyming slang).

kia ora
hello; g'day.

kick a goal
to have sexual intercourse.

kick 'er in the guts
encouragement to be more aggressive in order to get something moving or to get the required result.

kick for touch
avoid a major confrontation.

kicking tyres
talking about vehicles.

kick on
to continue, particularly when out on the town having a good time.

kick up bobsydie
to cause trouble.

kindy
kindergarten.

king pin
leading figure, 'big shot'.

kin oath/k'noath
   certainly.

kiss my arse
   an exclamation of disbelief.

Kiwi
   a New Zealander.

Kiwiana
   New Zealand collectibles.

Kiwified
   something or someone given New Zealand
   characteristics.

Kiwi fruit
   derogatory term for a
   homosexual New
   Zealander.

knock back
   to reject, as in 'I
   went to look for
   work but I was
   knocked back at
   every door.'

knock down
   to guzzle alcohol at
   great speed.

knockers
  breasts.

knock off
  to sell.

knock the wool out of one's head
  to make someone think straight.

knock up
  to make someone pregnant (vulgar use); to
  quickly make something, such as a cake or
  bookshelves.

know a thing or two
　　to be well-versed in matters, particularly of a
　　sexual nature.

knuckle sandwich
　　a punch in the mouth.

K Road
　　Karangahape Road in Auckland, cosmopolitan
　　by day, but mostly known for its seedier 'night
　　life'.

kumara
　　sweet potato.

L & P
　a lemon and paeroa soft drink.

ladies a plate
　plateful of food provided by a woman
　attending a social function.

lamb-brained
　stupid.

Land of the Long White Cloud/Shroud
　translation of Aotearoa, the Maori word for
　New Zealand.

land with your bum in butter
    to be very lucky.

larrikin
    lout, lovable troublemaker.

lash
    an attempt, as in 'Have a lash at this ball; see how far you can hit it.'

laughing gear
    mouth, as in 'Wrap your laughing gear around this ice-cream.'

lay a cable
    vulgar term for defecation.

lay an egg
get upset, as in 'Don't lay an egg, we'll get there on time.'

leftfooter
a Roman Catholic.

leg pull
to trick or hoax.

lemon-lipped
showing irritation on one's face.

length
vulgar term for penis, especially in its erect state.

left footer

let her rip
light-hearted command to get something moving, usually a vehicle.

lick, at full
at full speed.

lights are on, but nobody's home
said of a vague or stupid person.

like a blue-arsed fly
to be frantic.

like a fart in a fit
in a harried, agitated state.

like a maggot on the stove
  nervous; fidgety.

like a rat up a drainpipe
  very quick moving.

like a stunned mullet
  bewildered, inert.

like kissing your sister
  boring; uninspired.

like pushing shit uphill
  very difficult.

lip like a motherless foal
  sooky.

lippy
    shortened form of lipstick.

liquid amber
    beer.

liquid laugh
    an outpouring of vomit.

liquid lunch
    lunch consisting solely of alcohol.

little house
    toilet, commonly an outdoor one.

little lady
  wife.

little ripper
  excellent person or animal.

littlie
  a very young child.

live on birdseed
  to live or eat frugally.

log of wood
  idiotic person; the Ranfurly Shield.

long drop
  an outside toilet.

long tall streak of weasel piss
  a very skinny person.

looks like the back end of a wild pig
  very ugly.

loony bin
    psychiatric institution.

loosie
    a loose-forward in a rugby team.

lot, the
    a life sentence.

lower than shark shit
    despicable, as in 'Whoever ransacked this joint
    is lower than shark shit.'

luck of a Chinaman
    very lucky, with the derogatory implication
    (and racist undertone) that the person is not
    necessarily deserving of it.

lunatic soup
    alcohol.

lunchbox,
to open
one's
    to fart.

lurk
    a cunning and even
    illegal scheme to
    obtain money or some other benefit.

mad as a maggot/meat-axe
    eccentric.

maggot pack
    meat pie.

maimai
    a rough-and-ready shelter.

mainland, the
    the South Island.

make a box of
    to stuff something up.

make a quid
    to earn a living.

make a sale
    to vomit.

mango-tackle
    a tackle to the head.

Maori bunk
    a communal sleeping place.

Maori roast
    fish and chips.

Maori time
    to be unconcerned about time, as in 'Don't
    worry if you're late, mate, we're all on Maori
    time out here.'

market, to go to
    to become very angry or upset.

massive
    exclamation of full approval.

mate
    friend; common form of address, mainly
    between males.

mates' rates
    cheaper rates charged to friends when doing
    jobs for them.

Mick/Mickey Doolan
    a Catholic.

miffed
    annoyed, offended.

mingy
    mean, stingy.

miseryguts
    a sourpuss.

Mondayitis
    a fictitious disease due to a reluctance to return
    to work after the weekend.

money for jam
    easy money.

monty
    a sure thing.

moral
a certainty.

more arse than class
more energy than style.

more money than a bull can shit
extremely rich.

more than you could poke a stick at
a lot.

mosher
crowd surfer, particularly where loud music is playing.

mountain oysters
testicles from castrated lambs.

mouth like a yard of elastic
   a gossip.

mudguard
   derogatory term directed toward bald people.

mug
   one who is easily duped.

mug's game
   an unpleasant or unrewarding activity.

munted
   wiped out; destroyed.

murder house
   school dental clinic.

muttonfish
   paua.

muttonflaps
   vulgar term for women's genitalia.

mutton gun
   vulgar term for penis.

my arse is a red cabbage
   a statement of reassurance, as in 'If that's not
   the way it goes, my arse is a red cabbage.'

mystery parcel
   meat pie.

N

nail your hide to the dunny door
   threat of punishment.

nark
   to annoy someone; a spoilsport.

nasty piece of work
   an unpleasant individual.

naughty
   sexual intercourse,
   as in 'Did you
   do the
   naughty?'

Hi I'm Nick. Want a naughty!

neddy
a racehorse.

needs a good kick up the arse/bum
in need of punishment or discipline.

nervous burger
a cigarette.

never say die
surviving in the face of difficulties.

new chum
a newly arrived immigrant.

New Zealand Green
New Zealand-grown marijuana.

New Zild
New Zealand.

next bloke
an average bloke, as in 'Hey, I'm as decent as the next bloke, why won't you go out with me?'

nice one
a congratulatory statement, often after a good sporting move.

nick
to steal.

nick, in the
nude.

nick off/out/away
  to depart in a hurry.

nick over
  to quickly, and often on impulse, visit a friend.

night's a pup, the
  still very early.

ningnong/nong
  an idiot.

nipper
  a small child.

Nippon Clipon
  the Auckland Harbour Bridge.

nips on, to put the
  to ask for a loan of money.

no beg pardons
  full and aggressive play.

no brain surgeon
  not very smart.

no buts about it
  not for a matter of dispute.

no flies on (someone)
  said admiringly of a person, indicating quick-wittedness.

nohi
  nosey.

no hoper
  a hopeless person.

nose down, bum up
  very busy.

not a dog's show
  absolutely no chance.

nothing between the ears
  stupid.

not know your arse from your elbow, to
stupid or confused.

not much chop
not very good, as in 'That new teacher's not much chop, is she?'

not the full quid
not having full mental capacity.

not too foul
reasonably good.

no wucking furries
no f***ing worries; not a problem.

nuddy, in the
nude.

ocker
 an uncultured Australian
 man.

OE
 overseas experience.

*off like a robber's
dog/whore's
drawers*
 a hasty
 departure.

offside
 unpopular.

offsider
 assistant.

off your face
 stoned or drunk.

oil, the
 the gossip; the
 inside
 information.

ocker

old chook
  a silly old woman.

old chook

old hand
  an experienced person at a particular task.

old lady
  wife, girlfriend, or mother.

old man
  father.

olds
> parents, as in 'The olds have gone out; why don't you come over?'

on a bad trot
> a run of bad luck.

on a good wicket
> to be involved in a successful or non-stressful activity.

on a sticky wicket
> in trouble.

I'm in a spot of bother here!

one-armed bandit
> a poker machine operated by pulling a lever.

one-eyed trouser snake
> vulgar term for penis.

only got one oar in the water
    a daydreamer or incompetent individual.

on side
    to put oneself in a satisfactory position.

on the nose
    foul-smelling.

on the outer
    in the bad books.

on the turps
    drinking excessively, as in 'He's been on the turps ever since his wife left him.'

on with
to be romantically involved with.

open slather
no restrictions.

op shop
shortened form of opportunity shop, a place
which sells second-hand goods to raise money
for charity.

out of one's tree
totally drunk.

out of whack
not aligned correctly.

out on one's own
to be beyond reproach.

out to it
fast asleep; unconscious due to excessive
alcohol consumption.

over the fence
greedy.

Oz
Australia.

pack a sad
    displaying sadness.

pack a shitty
    to lose control of your temper.

pack of bludgers
    good-for-nothing group of people, as in 'Look
    at those pack of bludgers; they'll never get a
    job hanging around the pub all day.'

pack shit
    terrified.

pair
    breasts, as in 'Cor, she's got a pair!'

pair of bastards on a raft
    poached eggs on toast.

Pakeha
    a non-Maori New Zealander.

Palmie
    Palmerston North.

paralytic
  extremely intoxicated.

park your ears
  to listen to gossip.

part up
  to pay up.

pash
  to kiss passionately.

Pat Malone, to be on one's
  to be alone.

pav
  pavlova: a famous Australian/New Zealand
  dessert with a meringue base.

pay through the nose
to be charged excessively for a good or service, as in 'I had to pay through the nose to get the engine rebuilt.'

pearler
a fantastic person or thing.

perve
to stare lustfully.

pick
to guess correctly, as in 'Hey, mate, I picked the winner at the races!'

pickle me daisies!
exclamation of doubt.

pie-cart
a mobile eating place.

piece of piss
easy, as in 'Getting this job done is going to be a piece of piss.'

piker
someone who declines to go out or participate.

pill
a rugby ball.

pipped at the post
narrowly beaten.

piss
> alcohol; urine.

piss all over
> to defeat convincingly, as in 'We pissed all over them; they'll be too scared to play us again.'

piss awful
> very bad, as in 'I'm making a piss-awful mess of things in my new job.'

piss easy
> very easy, as in 'That test was piss-easy, mate.'

pissed as a parrot/pissed to the eyeballs
> completely inebriated.

pisser
> the pub.

pissfart
> to muck around, particularly in reference to wasting time, as in 'Stop pissfarting around and get to work.'

pisshead
> one who indulges in excessive alcohol consumption.

pissing down
> raining heavily.

pissing it up a wall
> wasting money on unimportant things.

piss in (someone's) pocket
    to ingratiate yourself with a person; to flatter.

piss in the wind
    not bringing a good outcome.

piss, to go on the
    to go on an alcohol binge.

pissy-eyed
    drunk.

plonk
    alcohol, usually of the cheaper variety.

point Percy at the porcelain (of a man)
to urinate.

poke
to have sexual intercourse from a man's point
of view, as in 'Harry poked Sheila every chance
he could get.'

poke a stick at, more than you can
an over-abundance of something.

poked
exhausted.

pokies
poker machines.

pollie
a politician.

polly
a Polynesian.

pom
an English person.

pong
a really bad smell.

POQ
piss off quick.

pork chop at a synagogue, to feel like a
to feel embarrassed, uneasy, or very out of
place.

porridge pot
a pool of boiling mud.

possie
position, as in 'That'd be a good possie to set
up the tent.'

prang
a car accident.

preggers
pregnant.

puckeroo
broken.

pull a swiftie
to deceive someone.

pull (someone's) leg/tit
to play a trick on; to tease; to joke.

pull your finger out
command to get a move on; hurry up.

pull your head in
command to mind your own business.

push shit uphill with a chopstick
 very difficult, as in 'Knocking that wall down
 was like pushing shit uphill with a chopstick!'

put a cork in it
 to shut up; be quiet.

put across a beauty
 a wise action.

put the boot in.
　　to attack, especially someone who is already
　　down.

put the hard word on.
　　to ask for a loan; to make an unwelcome
　　sexual suggestion.

put the shits up
　　to scare someone, as in 'I screamed in his ear
　　and put the shits up him.'

put up with
　　to endure.

put your kicking boots on
　　to set about doing something important.

py korry
　　by God.

quack
  a doctor.

quarter acre
  the once standard size
  of a house block.

Queen Street farmer
   a city businessman with a farm.

queer
   said of someone who is strange; mentally
   deficient.

quickie, to pull a
   to deceive someone.

quick smart
   immediately, as in 'I want you to tidy up that
   mess quick smart, young man!'

quid, not the full
   mentally deficient.

quids, would't miss it for
   a priceless moment or occasion, as in 'I
   wouldn't miss my son's rugby finals for quids.'

quiet, on the
   secretly; on the sly.

quince
   an effeminate man.

quite a few
   a lot, often in reference to beer.

quite nicely
   sufficient, as in 'Three more chairs for the
   guests to sit on will do quite nicely.'

quizzy
   to ask too many questions.

quoit
   buttocks.

quoit.

rabid
exceedingly angry.

rack off
go away; get lost.

Rafferty's rules
no rules at all.

raincoat
a condom.

rajah
vulgar term for an erect penis.

ram it down your throat
to be nagged or have something unwanted
forced upon you.

randy as a bitch on heat
very horny.

rapt
elated.

rare as hen's teeth
extremely rare.

rark up/rev up
  to incite or rebuke someone.

ratbag
  an annoying or eccentric person.

ratbaggery
  loutish, unacceptable behaviour.

rat-house
  mental institution.

rat shit
  of poor condition or quality, as in 'This is a rat shit paint job.'

rattletrap
  an old, rundown vehicle.

rattle your dags
  a command to hurry up.

ratty
  irritable.

razz
  to jeer.

ready-made
  a ready-made cigarette – one which has been bought from a store. Compare with a roll-your-own cigarette.

red as a beetroot
  to be embarrassed.

red collar
    to cut the throat of a sheep.

red sails in the sunset
    a vulgar term for menstruation.

rego
    car registration.

rellie
    a relation, as in 'We're having the rellies over
    for Christmas lunch this year.'

ring around that, put a
    a sure thing.

ringbark
    a vulgar term for circumcision, as in 'When
    Bluey had his kid ringbarked you shoulda
    heard him screaming!'

ring-in
    a substitution, as in 'They've gone and got a
    ring-in so they can win this game!'

rip into
    attack vigorously (either physically or
    verbally).

rip shit and bust
    to make a huge effort.

robber's dog, in like a
    very keen to participate.

rocket fuel
    alcohol.

roll-your-own
    a hand-rolled cigarette. Compare with a ready-
    made cigarette.

root
    to have sexual intercourse.

rooted
    totally exhausted.

ropeable
    violently angry.

rort
    a scam.

rough as a pig's breakfast/rough as guts
    without manners.

rubber guts
someone lacking braveness.

rubbish
to criticise, as in 'Hiwi's mum really rubbished his new girlfriend.'

rubbity-dub
rhyming slang for pub.

rug-rats
babies, toddlers.

rumble
a fight.

run around like a chook with its head cut off
to rush about ineffectually.

run-in
an argument.

run like a hairy goat
to perform badly in a race (usually said of a racehorse).

rustbucket
an old, worn-out car.

same diff
an expression meaning 'more or less of the same thing'.

same here
an expression of unqualified agreement.

sammie
a sandwich.

Samoan steroid
taro.

sandwich short of a picnic
lacking in intelligence.

save it
don't tell me, as in 'Save it, mate, I don't want to hear your excuses.'

scab
an abusive term for a non-union worker.

scarfie
    a student.

scanfies

scone, to do one's
    to become very angry.

scoot
    to depart in haste, as in 'I must scoot off now,
    I'm late for dinner.'

scratchie
an instant lottery ticket where a grey material must be scratched off in order to see if you've won a prize.

screaming heebie-jeebies
intense irritation, as in 'Someone dragging their fingernails down a blackboard really gives me the screaming heebie-jeebies.'

scum bag
a low-down, despicable individual.

scungy
filthy, greasy, repulsive.

search me
term meaning 'I don't know'. As in, 'Search me why John pissed off with Tony's wife.'

see you later
goodbye (said regardless of whether or not the speaker intends to see the other person later on.)

sell out
to vomit, particularly after overindulging in alcohol.

session
a drinking episode, as in 'Let's go have a session at the pub.'

sexo
a nymphomaniac; (in prisons) a sexual offender.

shaggin' wagon
a station wagon where a couple have sex.

shake your shirt
to get a move on, as in 'Shake your shirt and come over here!'

Shaky Isles
New Zealand.

shark and taties
fish and chips.

sheep shagger
an Australian.

sheila
a woman or girl.

shellacking
a brutal beating, either in sport or in a fight.

she'll be right
expression said to typify the easy-going Kiwi attitude.

she's on
said of a woman available for sex.

shickered
drunk.

shift along
to move with haste.

shit for brains
a stupid person.

shithouse
a lavatory; of poor quality; awful.

shit in
to win very easily.

shit of a thing
something unpleasant.

shitting bricks
to be furious or frightened.

shitty
irritable; of poor quality; awful.

shonky
unreliable; dishonest.

shoot through
to leave in a hurry (sometimes used to refer to
the father-to-be's desertion of his pregnant
girlfriend.)

short-arse
a person lacking in height.

short-fuse
quick-tempered.

short of change
mentally deficient.

shot full of holes
drunk.

shout
to pay for a treat of some sort; a round of drinks, as in 'Next time it's my shout!'

shrapnel
small change.

shrewdie
a cunning or deceptive person.

shut your neck
command to be quiet.

sickie, to throw a
to pretend to be ill so that you don't have to work.

sideways
suicide, as in 'The poor bastard's dad went out sideways.'

silly as a two-bob watch/silly as a wet hen
unreliable; crazy.

Silver Ferns
the New Zealand netball team.

sink the boot/sink the slipper
to kick viciously; to attack verbally.

skedaddle
to leave hastily.

skew-whift
askew.

skite
to show off.

skivvy
form of clothing made out of thin material,
similar to a long-sleeved t-shirt, but with a
high turtle-neck.

sling the dirt at
to slander someone.

slip
the remains of a landslide.

slog down
to gulp liquid - especially beer - quickly.

sly grog
alcohol sold illegally, particularly from an
unlicensed premises or after the pub's normal
closing time.

smart arse
an overly clever and disagreeable person.

smoko
short break from work for morning or afternoon tea.

snag/snarler
a sausage.

snaky
irritable.

sook
a cloying or cowardly individual; a wimp.

spanker
a dried cow patty used in dung fights.

sparky
an electrician.

sparrow's fart
just before dawn; very early.

spew
vomit (both the action of vomiting and vomit itself).

spit the dummy
to lose one's temper.

splash the boots
to urinate.

sponger
a person who lives off the generosity of others.

spoon
a fool.

spot on
completely right.

sprog
a child.

spud
to make pregnant.

spunk
a sexy, good-looking person.

squiz
to take a quick look at someone/something.

stand around like a stale bottle of piss
standing around at a loose end.

starkers
naked.

staunch
completely dependable and loyal.

stick like snot to a wall
loyal.

sticks out like a dog's balls
very clear; evident.

stick to your ribs, this will
    this will fill you up; a hearty meal, often
    containing meat and potatoes.

sticky beak
    an inquisitive or prying person.

stiff bickies
    too bad, as in 'You don't want to eat your
    veggies? Well, stiff bickies because you are
    going to!'

stiffie
    a vulgar term for an erection.

stirrer
    a troublemaker.

stone the crows
    an exclamation of surprise.

stonkered
    ruined.

strapped
    penniless, as in 'Mate, I'm a bit strapped for
    cash, could you lend me a buck or two?'

strewth
    an exclamation of surprise, said to be a
    contraction of 'In God's truth'.

stuffed
    ruined; exhausted.

stuff it up your jumper
command akin to 'Get lost!'

stuff-up
a mix-up or blunder.

suck the kumara
to die.

Sulphur City
Rotorua.

sunnies
sunglasses.

suss
suspicious.

sussed
worked out, as in 'Even though I haven't got the manual, I've got this thing sussed.'

swannie
a workman's shirt (a swandri).

sweet
good, fine, easy.

swifty, to pull a
a trick.

syphon the python
(of a man) to urinate.

taiho
   a command to wait.

take a punt
   to take a chance.

take the mickey out of
   to ridicule or tease.

Tall Blacks
   New Zealand's men's basketball team.

tall poppy
   a conspicuously successful person (often envied by others).

tanked
   drunk.

Taranaki sunshine
   rain.

Taranaki topdressing
   cow shit.

tatt
   a tattoo.

tear up for arsepaper
  to scold or admonish severely.

tee up
  to make an arrangement.

thick as a brick/thick as pig shit
  mentally deficient.

things you see when you don't have your gun
  a resigned comment, as in 'I'd love that suit but I left my wallet at home. Damn it, the things you see when you don't have your gun.'

thinks that the sun shines out of his/her arse
to have an exaggerated regard for oneself or
another person.

tight as a bull's/duck's/gnat's arse
very frugal with money.

tiki-tour
unlicensed driving; a scenic tour.

tin-bum/tinny-arse/tinny-bugger
terms used to describe someone who always
seems to have good luck.

tinnie
small amount of marijuana wrapped in
aluminium foil; a can of beer.

tits in a tangle, don't get your
don't get upset, as in 'Don't get your tits in a
tangle, love, I'll be there on time.'

toerag
an obnoxious person.

toey
  touchy.

togs
  a swimming costume.

too right
  an emphatic affirmative.

top shelf
  the very best.

toss your lollies
  to vomit.

tote up
  to add up.

tough bickies/tough titties
  bad luck, as in 'You wanted to have a go first? Well, tough bickies.'

town bike
  a promiscuous woman.

townie
  person living in a city or town.

tramping
  bushwalking.

troppo
  mad; eccentric.

trots
to suffer from diarrhoea, 'Gee, that curry really gave me the trots.'

true blue
the real thing.

turn in
to give up.

turn it on
to throw a party.

turn it up
command to be reasonable, 'You want me to come home by midnight? Turn it up!'

turps
any strong alcoholic drink; an abbreviation of turpentine.

twit
an idiot.

two kumaras short of a hangi
mentally deficient.

two men and a dog
very few people; a poor attendance.

two-thirds of five-eighths of f*** all
a tiny amount.

U

uglier than a cow facing south
very ugly.

underdungers/undies
underpants.

underground mutton
rabbit.

under the weather
drunk or tired.

uni
  shortened form of university.

up and under
  a rugby ball kicked very high into the air.

up oneself
  to be conceited, as in 'Gee, Ranji's brother is up himself!'

up shit creek without a paddle
  in serious trouble.

up the chute
to be wrong.

up the duff
vulgar term for
being pregnant.

upya
shortened (slightly
more polite term)
for up your arse.

*up your nose with
a rubber hose*
said as a firm
rejection.

ute
a utility truck.

Don't be vulgar!

vag
    vagrant.

varsity
    university.

Vee-dub
    a Volkswagen.

veggie
    shortened form of vegetable.

verandah above the toyshop
a male paunch.

verbal diarrhoea
   excessive talking.

very funny
   said to mean the opposite, as in 'The rugby's on and we're all out of beer? Very funny!'

vid
   video.

village bike
   a promiscuous woman.

Vinnies, The
   the St Vincent de Paul Catholic charity.

vitamin DB
   Dominion Breweries draught bitter.

vollie
   a volunteer.

waddy
   a heavy stick or club.

wahine
   woman or wife.

Waikikamukau
   one of many fictional place names to denote a
   rural place.

Waka blonde
   a Maori woman.

wally
   an idiot; a classic short-back-and-sides haircut.

Way Down Under
   New Zealand.

weak as cat's piss
   ineffectual; feeble.

weekend root
   casual sexual partner.

well gone
   head over heels in love.

were you born in a tent?
    sarcastic question asked of a person who
    habitually leaves the door open.

west coaster
    one born or raised on the west coast of the
    South Island.

westie
    someone from the western suburbs of
    Auckland.

whack up
   to cook or bake at short notice, as in 'I'll just whack up some scones and we'll have morning tea.'

whale into
   to attack brutally.

what are ya?
   sarcastic exclamation said when someone says something foolish.

whatcha-m'-call-it/whaddya-call-it?
   a term used for any object/concept that you don't know the name of.

what do you do for a crust?
   meaning 'What do you do for a living?'

what's the damage?
   meaning 'How much do I owe you?'

when the shit hits the fan
   when a problem or mistake comes out into the open and reaches it's peak.

whinge
   to whine; a whining complaint.

whips of
   plenty of, as in 'There's whips of ice-cream here; have as much as you want.'

whip the cat
   to complain or reproach oneself.

whirl, give it a
to try; make an effort.

whole box and dice
everything.

whopper
anything enormous; a huge lie.

who's milking the cow?
question akin to 'Who's in charge here?'

Windy City
Wellington.

within cooee
quite a close distance.

wobbly, to chuck a
to throw a tantrum, as in 'She chucked a wobbly when I said I was breaking our date.'

wonky
unsteady; shaky.

wooden Aspro
a police truncheon.

wop-wops
a remote area.

working for the prime minister
on welfare.

would bet on two flies walking up the wall
said of a compulsive gambler.

wouldn't give you the time of day
said of an uncooperative, stand-offish or mean person.

wouldn't know his arse from his elbow/wouldn't know shit from clay unless he tasted it
said of a very stupid person.

wouldn't work in an iron lung
a lazy person.

would shit anywhere
a mannerless person.

wowser
a killjoy; one who disapproves of drinking, gambling and dancing.

wrung out like a dishcloth
utterly exhausted.

WWW
World Wide Wait. A play on World Wide Web; the frustratingly long time it can take to surf the Internet.

yachtie
a yachtsman.

yahooing
behaving in a loutish manner.

yakka
work, as in 'This dirt-shovelling is bloody hard yakka.'

yank tank
a large American vehicle.

yarn
to tell stories.

yobbo
a lout.

yodel
to vomit.

yonks
a long time, as in 'Great to see you mate! Haven't seen you around here for yonks!'

you ain't wrong
you're right.

you beaut/you little beauty
a jubilant exclamation, as in 'You beaut! My horse came in first!'

your blood's worth bottling
said to someone one admires, or to one who has done something excellent.

your shout
your turn to buy a round of drinks.

you think you're a flowerpot because you've got a hole in your bum
you love yourself.

zack, *not worth a*
useless or worthless (sixpence in pre-decimal currency).

zambuck
a St John Ambulance officer.

zonk
idiot.

zonked
rendered paralytic by alcohol, overwork, or both.

Great

KIWI

Insults

You'll never truly have a grasp of the Kiwi language until you learn the various insults used in this fine country. On the following pages, different types of insults have been categorised accordingly, so an appropriate insult can be found for almost any occasion.

TO THE COMPLETELY STUPID

You couldn't hit a dead bull's bum with a tin can.

Not all your dogs are barking.

Not all your chooks are clucking.

You're not playing with the full deck.

You're not the full packet of Tim Tams.

You're not the full quid.

You're a few sprinkles short of a fairy bread sandwich.

You're as thick as the dust on a public servant's out-tray.

You're not the full two bob.

You wouldn't shout in a shark attack.

You're not worth a rat's arse.

You've got nothing between the ears.

You're going through life with the porch lights on dim.

You're a lettuce leaf short of a salad.

You're as silly as a wet hen.

You're a few peanuts short of a jar of peanut butter.

You're so slow you couldn't get a job as a speed hump.

You're so wet I could shoot ducks off you.

You're as thick as a brick.

You've only got one oar in the water.

You're a patient short of a funny farm.

You're as bright as a two-watt bulb.

You couldn't run guts for a slow butcher.

You're so dense you drive uphill with the clutch slipping.

When God was handing out brains you were out chewing your cud with the cows.

You're a brick short of a load.

You're a few stubbies short of a six-pack.

You've got space to sell between your ears, but no one wants to buy it.

You haven't got all four paws on the mouse.

Your lift doesn't go all the way to the top floor.

If your brains were dynamite you couldn't blow your hat off.

Your lights are on but there's nobody home.

You've got only fifty cards in the pack.

You're short of numbers in the Upper House.

You're a snag short of a barbecue.

When God was handing out brains you were busy counting stones in the gravel.

If your brains were dynamite you wouldn't have enough to part your hair.

You wouldn't know your arse from your elbow.

You're a slice short of a loaf.

You wouldn't know a sheep from your wife.

You're up the pole, mate!

You couldn't pick out the colour white in a snowstorm.

If your brains were dynamite you couldn't blow your eyebrows off.

You couldn't organise a fart in a baked beans factory.

You der!

You couldn't organise a wet t-shirt competition if you were at the Playboy Mansion.

You're a ningnong.

If your brains were made of elastic they wouldn't make a set of garters for a one-legged budgie.

You wouldn't know if a band was up ya until you got the drum.

You couldn't run out of sight on a dark night.

You wouldn't know whether it's Queen Street or Christmas.

You're a dingdong.

Watch out – if you pick your nose your head will cave in.

You haven't got enough brains to give yourself a headache.

You've got shit for brains.

You haven't got enough sense to come in out of the rain.

If your brains were dynamite you couldn't blow your hat off.

If your brains were shit you wouldn't have enough to soil your tie.

If you were given a brain it would be lonely.

You're not firing on all cylinders.

You're an egg salad sandwich short of a picnic.

You can see daylight through your ears.

You're a shingle short.

You're a twit.

You're short of a sheet of bark.

You're as slow as a paralysed turtle.

You're as silly as a tin of worms.

You wouldn't know if a bus was up ya till the people got off.

You're as silly as a two-bob watch.

You're as silly as a solar-powered torch.

Your IQ is way below room temperature.

You're as slow as a wet hen.

You're as slow as a wet week.

You wouldn't know if a train was up ya till the whistle blew.

You've got the IQ of a green banana.

You're a bit slow off the mark.

You went to the race, but you forgot to leave the start line.

You're a sally.

You're soft in the crumpet.

You're a drongo.

You've got a brain like a cow's udder.

You're ten cents short of the dollar.

You're a dingbat.

You're an umbrella short of a cocktail.

You're as thick as two short planks.

You wouldn't know if a tram was up ya till the conductor started checking your tickets.

You're a wally.

You wouldn't know your arse from a hole in a flowerpot.

You're as thick as pig shit.

You're a dill.

If your brains were shit, you wouldn't need any toilet paper.

If you had another brain, you could start a rock garden.

You're a gink.

You couldn't see the road to the dunny if it had red flags on it.

You're a nong.

You couldn't catch a cold if you sat naked all night in an icy pond.

You couldn't kick a hen off its nest.

You couldn't piss out of a boot with the directions written on the tongue.

You're a dropkick.

You couldn't sell a statue to a pigeon.

You're a dingaling.

You're not the full packet of Skittles.

TO THE UTTERLY PSYCHO

You've been touched in the head, and I think it was with a jackhammer.

You're as nutty as a date loaf.

You're off your nana.

You're off your rocker.

You fell off the merry-go-round and they're not gonna let you back on it!

You're as mad as a cut snake.

You're up the pole.

You're as mad as a hatter.

You're around the twist.

You're as barmy as a bandicoot.

You're bats.

You've got bats in your belfry.

You're as bent as a scrub tick.

You're bonkers.

You're berko.

You've got some palings off the fence.

You've got white ants in the woodwork.

You've got kangaroos in your top paddock.

You've got nits in the network.

You're a loony.

You're as mad as a maggot.

You're as mad as a meat axe.

You're wacko.

There's mould in your fridge and you're cooking it for dinner.

You're touched.

You're troppo.

TO THE DOWNRIGHT USELESS

You're as useful as a one-legged man in an arse-kicking contest.

You couldn't knock the skin off a rice pudding.

You couldn't give away presents at an orphanage at Christmas time.

You're as useful as a flywire door on a submarine.

You're not worth a pinch of goat shit.

You couldn't give away cheese at a rats' picnic.

You couldn't give away condoms to a rugby team partying with a bunch of supermodels.

You couldn't last a round in a revolving door.

You couldn't run a chook raffle in a country pub.

You couldn't train a passionfruit vine over a country dunny.

You couldn't win if you started the night before.

You must have got your licence out of a Cornflakes packet.

You've only got one oar in the water.

You're so wet you could shoot ducks off you.

You're as weak as a wet whistle.

You're as weak as cat piss.

You couldn't fart into a bottle.

You couldn't fight your way out of a paper bag.

You couldn't hit the side of a barn.

You couldn't get a kick in a stampede.

You couldn't hit a cow in the tit with a tin can.

You're a no hoper.

TO THE HORRIFICALLY UGLY

You're all behind in Auckland (meaning you have a rather large posterior).

You've got teeth like a row of condemned houses.

I've seen better heads on a bumful of boils.

You've got a head like a Mini with the doors open.

You could open a can of peaches with that nose.

You could eat an apple through a picket fence.

I've seen better heads on a glass of beer.

I've seen better heads on a back full of acne.

You've got hair like a dunny brush and shitty breath to match.

You're as bald as a bandicoot.

You've got a verandah above the toyshop.

You've got hair like a bush pig's arse.

You're as skinny as a sapling with the bark scraped off.

That zit on your nose sticks out like a dog's balls.

Your great big honker stands out like a black crow in a bucket of milk.

You're broad in the beam.

Your head is like a robber's dog.

Your thighs wouldn't stop a pig in a hall.

What time are you leaving, barge arse?

TO THE PLAIN DRUNK

You're belly dancing with the hippos.

You're away with the pixies.

You're blind.

You're as full as a fairy's phone book.

You're as full as a fat woman's sock.

You're smashed.

You're as full as a state school.

You're as full as a tick.

You're as full as a fat woman's underwear.

You're lit up like a Christmas tree.

You're more loaded than a fully loaded gun.

You're as pissed as a possum.

You're as pissed as a parrot.

You're as full as a boot.

You're out to it.

You're paralytic.

You're as pissed as a newt.

You're as rotten as a chop.

You're shot full of holes.

You've got a mouth like a camel-driver's crutch.

You're a two-pot screamer.

You're two and a half sheets to the wind.

You're shickered, shellacked and shit-faced as well.

You're a pisspot.

Your mouth's like the bottom of a cocky's cage.

You're under the weather.

TO THE MEAN AND STINGY

You're so stingy you wouldn't give someone the steam off your shit.

You're so stingy that when a fly lands in the sugar you shake it before you kill it.

You're as tight as a fish's arse.

You're as mean as bird shit.

You're so stingy that you wouldn't give a rat a railway pie.

You're as tight as a bull's arse in fly time.

You're so stingy that if a fly walked over your butter you'd lick the fly before you killed it.

GENERAL ALL-PURPOSE NASTY PHRASES

You give me the Jimmy Brits! (Rhyming slang for the shits.)

Go and take a running jump at yourself.

You're a nasty piece of bacon gristle.

I wouldn't piss on you if you were on fire.

I wouldn't jump on you if you were a trampoline.

I'll knock your teeth so far down your throat you'll have to stick a toothbrush up your arse to clean them!

Just cleaning my teeth dear!

You're nosey enough to want to know the ins and outs of a chook's bum.

I wouldn't piss down your throat if your guts were on fire.

Up your arse with a piece of glass!

You'd bore the hair off a gay man's moustache.

Pull your head in!

Put a sock in it!

Put a cork in it!

What do you think this is – bush week?

What the bloody hell's crawlin' on you, mate?

You wacker!

Go bite your bum!

You're an arsehole.

You're a scunge bag.

You're a nasty piece of work.

You're a grizzleguts.

You're lower than a snake's belly.

You're a scumbag.

I wouldn't use you for sharkbait.

I wouldn't piss on you if you were on fire.

You'd made a blowfly sick!

You're a suck.

Go bite your bum.

Kiss my arse.

You're a toerag.

You're an arse-licker.

Do me a favour...

You're all piss and wind.

You're a big girl's blouse.

You're as cunning as a Maori's dog.

Shut your neck.

You give me the shits.

Get off the grass.

Up your nose with a rubber hose.

Stiff bickies.

You're a ratbag.

Go to buggery.

Tough titty.